FORGIVE TO LIVE

TO

WORKBOOK

FORGIVE TO LIVE

TO

WORKBOOK

HOW FORGIVENESS CAN SAVE YOUR LIFE

DR. DICK TIBBITS
WITH STEVE HALLIDAY

INTEGRITY®
PUBLISHERS
Nashville

FLORIDA
HOSPITAL

BOOKS BY DR. DICK TIBBITS

Forgive to Live

Forgive to Live Workbook

Forgive to Live Devotional

ALSO BY DR. DICK TIBBITS

Forgive to Live Video Curriculum

FORGIVE TO LIVE WORKBOOK

Copyright © 2006 Dick Tibbits

Published by Integrity Publishers, a division of Integrity Media, Inc.
660 Bakers Bridge Avenue, Franklin, TN 37067

HELPING PEOPLE WORLDWIDE EXPERIENCE *the* MANIFEST PRESENCE *of* GOD

PUBLISHER'S NOTE: This workbook is not intended to replace a one-on-one relationship with a qualified health-care professional, but as a sharing of knowledge and information from the research and experience of the author. You are advised and encouraged to consult with your health-care professional in all matters relating to your health and the health of your family. The publisher and author disclaim any liability arising directly or indirectly from the use of this workbook.

AUTHOR'S NOTE: This workbook contains numerous case histories and patient stories. In order to preserve the privacy of the people involved, I have disguised their names, physical appearance, and aspects of their personal stories so that they are not identifiable. Case histories may also include composite characters.

General Editor, Florida Hospital: Todd Chobotar
Florida Hospital Review Board: Ernie Bursey, Debbie Pusateri, Richard Duerksen
Photography: Spencer Freeman
Illustrations by: Red Hughes
Cover Design by: Russ McIntosh, Brand Navigation, LLC, www.brandnavigation.com
Interior Design by: Rainbow Graphics

Published in association with the literary agency of Alive Communications, Inc.
7680 Goddard St, Suite 200, Colorado Springs, CO 80920

ISBN-13: 9-781-59145-471-7
ISBN-10: 1-59145-471-9 (tradepaper workbook)

Printed in the United States of America
06 07 08 09 10 VP 9 8 7 6 5 4 3 2 1

CONTENTS

INTRODUCTION

For several years I have been conducting "Forgive for Life" seminars across the country, teaching participants the nuts and bolts of forgiveness as a way to improve their physical, mental, and spiritual health. The book *Forgive to Live* grew out of these seminars—as did a scientific study that shows how forgiveness training can actually lower blood pressure. In this companion workbook I have attempted to present the core content of the book and seminar so that you can experience for yourself the powerful benefits of forgiveness.

This workbook may be used either in conjunction with *Forgive to Live* or on its own.[1] The book covers the topics in much greater detail than is possible here and will greatly enhance your learning experience, but the workbook does present the material necessary for you to begin your journey toward forgiveness. This workbook also provides opportunities for further insight into forgiveness and the practical application of what you learn.

---

[1] The book has twelve chapters, but this workbook has only eight. The following chart shows how chapters in each volume correspond to one another:

	Workbook	Book
Chapters	1	1, 2
	2	5
	3	Introduction, 6
	4	7, 8
	5	9
	6	3
	7	4
	8	10, 12

The organization of the workbook more closely resembles my "Forgive for Life" seminars than the book. I have done this in order to get readers to the hands-on material as quickly as possible.

Each of the following eight chapters is divided into four main sections:

1. *Case Study*. To introduce the chapter, I begin with a case study, based on life experience of a real person.

2. *What You Need to Know*. In this section you'll find core information about the particular aspect of forgiveness under consideration. Occasional questions will help drive a point home.

3. *Tapping Into the Power of Forgiveness*. Here I present relevant exercises for you to do, additional questions for you to answer, and specific steps for you to take in order to enjoy the amazing benefits of forgiveness for yourself.

4. *Revisiting [Character's] Story*: In this final section I ask you to think through how what you've learned in this chapter could help the opening story's character—and you—move further along in the forgiveness journey.

You can use this workbook either on your own or with others in a discussion group. My goal is to help you get moving on the road to forgiveness so that you can leave behind the terrible hurts of the past and take positive steps toward the future you've always wanted.

I wish you all the best as you travel the path of forgiveness toward the bright tomorrow it offers you.

FORGIVENESS: A BASIC DEFINITION

Key to being able to forgive is understanding what forgiveness is—and what it isn't. First, what forgiveness is not.

Forgiveness is not forgetting.

Forgiveness is not excusing another's action.

Forgiveness is not necessarily reconciling.

Forgiveness is not intended to set others free.

More to come on this in the workbook. But if forgiveness is not pardoning, condoning, excusing, forgetting, denying, or even reconciling, then what is it? How can genuine forgiveness best be defined and understood so that it can do its amazing work of healing in your life?

Here's the definition I will use in this workbook:

> *Forgiveness is the process of reframing one's anger and hurt from the past, with the goal of recovering one's peace in the present and revitalizing one's purpose and hopes for the future.*

When you look closely at this definition, you'll see that the forgiveness process can be divided into three distinct phases:

- Phase 1: How I handle the memories of painful things said and done to me in the past

- Phase 2: How I overcome the negative emotions I feel right now

- Phase 3: How I free myself from a hurtful past to achieve my desired future

This workbook will help you understand and practice these necessary aspects of forgiving. After all, without covering the full range of past, present, and future, your forgiveness will be incomplete, making it much more difficult for you to experience a full and satisfying life.

TEN PRINCIPLES OF FORGIVENESS

Forgiveness begins when you . . .

1. Accept that life is not fair and that others may play by a different set of rules than you do

2. Stop blaming others for your circumstances

3. Understand that you cannot change the person who hurt you; you can only change yourself

4. Acknowledge the anger and hurt that some unpleasant or even harmful event is causing you

5. Reframe your story of hurt—your "grievance story"—by placing the hurtful events in a broader context than your current point of view

6. Recognize that only you can make the choice to forgive

7. Shift your view of the offender by humbly choosing to empathize with his or her life situation

8. Intentionally move from discontent toward contentment

9. Understand that forgiveness will take time and cannot be rushed

10. Take responsibility for your life and your future

If you want to live, at some point you must choose to forgive.

*R*obert worked tirelessly for his company. Whenever a project needed to get finished, he would stay on task until it shipped— always ahead of schedule. He consistently received stellar performance evaluations. So, as his supervisor's retirement drew near, Robert just knew he was in line for the job—and then it happened.

Robert's supervisor wanted a certain friend of his to replace him, so he told several lies that got Robert placed on probation. Since company policy did not allow anyone to be promoted while on probation, Robert was passed over when the supervisor retired. Through absolutely no fault of his own, Robert missed out on the promotion.

Robert's anger over the unfair incident soon began to ruin his life. To bury his rage, Robert started to drink heavily. As a result, he frequently missed work, something that had never happened before. Within a few weeks, Robert got fired—and he blames his former supervisor for his dismissal.

WHAT YOU NEED TO KNOW

We all want to believe that life should be fair. If, like Robert, we work hard, complete our assignments, and produce for the company, we should get the promotion we deserve. But what happens when that promotion doesn't come, when life turns out not to be so fair after all? How can we best respond to the unfair things that happen to us?

When hurtful things happen to us, most of us tend to respond in predictable ways:

- We try to win an apology.

- We feel additional hurt when the other person doesn't respond in helpful ways.

- Our hurt turns into anger and then into resentment.

- We start to fantasize about revenge even though it is unlikely we will ever follow through with our plan.

- We withdraw from the person who hurt us and maybe even from life in general.

Basically, when life isn't fair, all of us have two choices.

We can either blame or forgive.

Blame says:

- What happened is your fault.

- Therefore, the misery in my life is your fault.

- In short, my life is your fault.

The reality is that blame doesn't solve problems; it only points a finger. And when you point your finger at someone else, the only possible solution to your problem is for that person to change. Blame maintains that, until that person changes, there is nothing you can do—and such a line of reasoning breeds helplessness.

Whenever you tell yourself that your misery is someone else's fault, you are opting for blame rather than choosing to forgive. You are, in effect, saying that the solution lies outside yourself and in the hands of someone else. I develop this thought more thoroughly in the book *Forgive to Live* showing how often we use blame to explain why our current circumstances are what they are. In short: my life is your fault. Finally, by allowing us to avoid taking responsibility, blame keeps us stuck in the past without any plan for improving our future.

You may, however, be surprised to read that blame is not all bad. Think back to Robert's situation. Suppose he believed that it was totally his fault he didn't get the promotion. That would simply not be true. So, while it's a problem to blame everything on the other person, it is equally a problem to blame everything on yourself.

It's very hard to assure equality . . . Some men are killed in war, others are wounded, and some never leave the country.

— John F. Kennedy

Forgiveness does not balance the scales of justice any more than vengeance does. But it will keep your past from destroying your future.

Furthermore, if you don't blame someone else for the bad thing that happened to you, then you have no one to forgive. So blame can be helpful in that it *focuses* our forgiveness; blame becomes detrimental only when you get stuck in it. At some point, you have to take responsibility for your life and take the necessary steps to make it better. Forgiveness is that first step.

Of course there will always be some bad in the world, but if you allow that unpleasant fact to paralyze you, then you will spend the rest of your life immobilized leaving you unable to deal with painful situations.

1. Summarize why blame is not a great way to deal with your hurt.*

---

* Throughout the book, this icon indicates questions that you may find appropriate for group discussion.

2. In spite of the fact that blame does not solve problems, why do you think most people choose that approach?

Clearly, forgiveness offers you a very different approach to life. While blame focuses on the hurt of the past and wishes life could be better, forgiveness teaches you to accept what you cannot change. It gives you the opportunity to move ahead despite the pain of your past. Forgiveness insists that vengeance always hurts you more than it does the person who hurt you. And forgiveness can help you move on and get past the problem. Know, however, that forgiveness will take time and it requires some difficult work today.

3. Look back at the definition of forgiveness on page XI as well as at the preceding paragraph. What aspect of forgiveness discussed in these two sections do you find most helpful? Why?

Tapping Into the Power of Forgiveness

When a wrong has been committed against you, how do you tend to respond? Do you . . .

- Figure out whom to blame

- Spend most of your time thinking about how to get even

- Think about how to make things right again

- Say, "Problem? What problem?" and deny that a wrong has been committed

4. Now think about a specific situation that still causes you pain and for which you blame another person. Briefly describe what happened.

Did you try to win an apology from the person? If not, why not? If so, what happened?

Do you feel resentful about the situation? How did those feelings affect you?

When life isn't fair, we are left with two choices: to blame or to forgive.

What fantasies of revenge have you entertained?

In what ways have you withdrawn from this person—or even from people—as a result of the hurtful event? Be specific.

5. What do you think could be done to make your situation right? To help you begin to answer that question, note which of the following best describes your most frequent thoughts.

The offender will eventually see how wrong he or she was and apologize.

The offender will be punished by either me or someone else.

I will go through the judicial process to get what I am owed.

I wish the whole situation would somehow just go away.

I hope to make new friends so I can forget this ugly incident.

I will forgive the person and move on with my life.

To minimize your disappointments, lower your expectations of people. Accepting the following two basic truths will help you do just that:
(1) People will make mistakes.
(2) People do not have to do what you want them to do.

6. Often we feel deeply hurt because we take what happened too personally. One way to prepare yourself for the healing power of forgiveness is to learn to take what happened less personally. So try to look at what this person did as a reflection of who he or she is. The other person's actions may have little to do with you and a whole lot to do with the way he or she treats everyone.

Does this person tend to act this way toward everyone, not just toward you? Give an example.

What do you think happened in the offender's past that caused him or her to act this way?

Could this person know exactly how his or her actions affected you? Explain.

The closer the relationship, the stronger the impact of the offense. For example, if a perfect stranger says to you, "That didn't make sense," you would most likely move on fairly easily, saying to yourself, "What does he know?" But if your best friend made the same statement, you might obsess about why she said such a thing to you. After all, you've talked about this before, so what did she really mean?

7. Discuss ways you can depersonalize comments other people make about you so that you will not be so deeply hurt.

8. You may feel that no one has suffered as you have, but realize that all the time thousands of people are suffering in similar ways. Why is this truth helpful?

9. Most of us initially resist the impulse to forgive. Which of the following best describes your hesitation about offering forgiveness to the one who hurt you?

I will not trust that person again.

I do not see how that person's repentance can be genuine after what he/she did to me.

I fear the person will repeat the hurtful behavior.

I have not been repaid, so that person's debt remains.

10. Continuously blaming others for your problems makes you a helpless victim, and clinging too strongly to that role defeats just one person: you. Keeping that fact in mind, answer the following questions:

If I wanted to portray myself as a victim, what points of my story would I emphasize?

The Declaration of Independence does not give you the right to happiness; it merely gives you the right to pursue happiness. Only you can make you happy.

In order to have any control over making my life better, I must consider who the primary actor in my story is. If I'm not taking that role, why would I think the other person who has the power will act in my best interest. So what can I do to become the primary actor in my story and get back in charge of my life?

Now for some pointers to get you moving on the road to forgiveness.

11. Give up all-or-nothing thinking about the person who hurt you.

    All people are a mixture of good and bad. Think, for instance, about someone you once liked but don't like as much anymore. When you liked that individual, you noticed all the good qualities—and then you got hurt. Now you see that same person as bad, and you notice only the negative traits. This same person has changed from good to bad because of the characteristics you choose to pay attention to. Also, consider that while you currently see that person as bad, someone else sees him or her as good.

    Why is it tempting to indulge in all-or-nothing thinking about someone who has hurt you?

In what ways have you been seeing the person who hurt you as all bad?

What good qualities might that person actually have?

Why is it simply inaccurate to see this person—any person—as all bad?

12. Distinguish between intent and impact.

Anytime a wrong has been done, we must address two issues: the intent (why those who hurt or offended us did what they did) and the impact (how those actions affected us). We can never be absolutely sure of the intent (the person's motives). Nevertheless, after we are hurt, most of our thoughts and emotions focus on intent, which we can know the least about, rather than on impact, about which we can be very clear.

Why is it important to distinguish between intent and impact when you're thinking about an unfair event in your life?

Why someone did something to us is often more important to us than *what* they actually did. Why do you think this is so?

What can you say about the wrongful situation you experienced that will acknowledge the hurt you feel (the impact) without providing a motive that you cannot confirm (the intent)? Someone in your small group may be able to offer you some thoughts from the offender's perspective that you haven't considered.

13. Reduce your expectations of others.

I expect more from someone I know than I do from a perfect stranger. This can mean heightened disappointment when the actions of my family, friends, neighbors, and co-workers do not meet my expectations.

Many times we feel hurt because we expect a person to do something that, in fact, we have no right to expect. What can you do to begin to reduce your expectations of others?

Why does lowering your expectations of others help you? When might having lower expectations of people be a problem for you?

Revisiting Robert's Problem

Life is like a game of cards. You have no control over what you're dealt—but you have full control over how you play your hand. Forgiveness is a way of playing a bad hand well.

All of us think life should be fair, but we have to realize that fairness is often in the eyes of the beholder. Consider Robert's case. What Robert experienced as an injustice, his boss saw as an opportunity to help a friend. So what was clearly detrimental to Robert and unfair to him was *not* all bad from another perspective.

What do you think Robert might have done if the roles had been reversed, if he had been in his boss's place? Although nothing can excuse the actions of Robert's boss, the answer to this question could free Robert from giving up and believing that he will never have a chance at another promotion.

If forgiveness just hasn't "worked" for you, could it be that you've been going about it the wrong way? Maybe you've mistaken the real thing for a widely accepted—but totally flawed—substitute.

Robert will need to take responsibility for his current thoughts and actions. Robert has the right, for instance, to pursue his concerns either with his boss's boss or through employee relations to be sure that no laws were violated. He gains nothing, however, by blaming others for the way his life currently is. Specifically, he needs to realize that his angry response all but assures that he will not be promoted in the future at some other job—and, without question, that will *not* be his former boss's doing.

Now answer a few questions:

14. What would you recommend Robert do to stop his suffering?

15. Who is Robert trying to punish by his actions? Is he accomplishing that goal? Explain.

16. Robert is spending more time being angry with his former boss than planning how he could grow his career. What can he do to get back on track?

17. Has Robert's anger at his boss changed anything? Is Robert's anger likely to change anything in the future? Explain.

18. Should Robert consider forgiveness a viable choice in his situation? Why or why not?

*J*ill married the week after her high school graduation. Her twenty-seven-year-old husband, Tom, held a minimum-wage job and he had been married once before. Jill's parents advised her to wait till after college before getting married. They were not too fond of Tom and felt their little girl wasn't mature enough to tie the knot. But love is blind.

Shortly after the wedding, Jill discovered Tom had an addiction to drugs; that is why he could never hold a job. Money issues soon overwhelmed the couple. They suffered under a mounting pile of debt and always seemed on the verge of being evicted from their apartment. And then, to top everything off, Jill became pregnant.

The couple's fighting increased, and with no solution to any of their problems in sight, they simply argued more often and more viciously. Always one to avoid conflict, Tom started spending more time away from home and at the bar. Before long Jill suspected he was seeing someone else—a suspicion that proved accurate when she discovered notes from Tom's girlfriend and some compromising pictures in his wallet.

Jill tearfully filed for divorce. With no job, no marketable skills, and a baby daughter to care for, she considered her life a total shambles.

Ten years later, Jill is still scraping by. If you talk to her, you'll soon hear the whole, sordid story about how Tom ruined her life.

WHAT YOU NEED TO KNOW

Our lives are largely the result of the stories we believe. If, for example, we continually tell ourselves that someone has ruined our life, then we will probably allow that story to totally destroy our life.

When something hurtful happens to you and you stew over the problem more than is necessary, you are creating a grievance story (a concept further developed and explained in the book *Forgive to Live*). This tale of helplessness explains your inability to improve your life. It also causes you to spend more time thinking about what is wrong with your life than about what you could do to improve it. In short, you hand over a ton of energy and a tremendous amount of mental real estate to someone you don't even like.

A grievance story develops when you:

Forgiveness does not wipe out your memory, nor is it a delete key for reality. The test of genuine forgiveness is not whether you remember the event, but how you remember it.

- Suffer some kind of wrong

- Attach a specific—and heavily negative—interpretation to the event

- Take the offense personally

- Frequently retell the story to yourself and to others

1. Write out your grievance story. This is the story of someone who caused you great harm or deep pain.

   Who is the main character in your story: you or the one who hurt you?

   What affect does this story have on you every time you retell it?

   Why do you frequently tell the story?

   What are you hoping to gain with each retelling of the story?

*If you are
distressed by
anything external,
the pain is not due
to the thing itself,
but to your
estimate of it; and
this you have the
power to revoke at
any moment.*

— *Marcus Antonius*

Telling and retelling your grievance story does not heal your injury. In fact, it actually reopens old wounds and often makes them worse. Grievance stories fuel grudges, which consume your life, deplete your energy (that you could better spend on more important activities), and make you feel the old pain with even greater intensity. If you're like most people, you tell and retell your grievance story, fantasizing that somehow the one who hurt you will accept your point of view and change things to make your life better. But almost always the one who suffers most by its retelling is not the offender from the past, but you, your family, and your friends in the present.

If you want to move toward health, you have to acknowledge that the past exists only in your memory. It has power over your life only as long as you recall it and thereby relive it in the present. When you do this, you feel all the painful feelings anew, and that's why you live as if the hurtful event were a present-day reality. In short, you hurt yourself over and over again.

*Your life is
profoundly
influenced by the
stories you
believe—
including the stories
you tell yourself.*

Consider two more problems with your grievance story. First, while you see its account of things as reality, your story actually is a distortion of the true and larger picture. In fact, that distortion is key to its power to entrap you. Second, the offender in your story is the one who controls the action; you cast yourself as little more than a powerless victim. So as long as you repeat your grievance story, you're telling yourself a lie that leaves you feeling helpless to make any changes for the better.

2. Why is your grievance story able to pass itself off as reality?

3. In what specific ways might your own grievance story be distorting reality?

4. What evil motives does your grievance story assign to the person who hurt you?

Never repeat old grievances.

— Ancient proverb

Forgiveness allows you to reframe your story, thus changing its essence, enabling you to see life from a different perspective, and leading you to a healthier and more satisfying life.

Here's the real truth: you are not chained to your past, nor is your future determined by your past. Forgiveness helps you revise your grievance story so that it more accurately reflects reality and therefore enables you to leave the hurtful past behind and stride confidently into a hope-filled future. Forgiveness also teaches you that:

- Holding on to your anger hurts you more than anyone else

- You set yourself free by forgiving the person who hurt you

- When you change for the better, people around you more easily change for the better

Save your energy and best thoughts for people who help you, encourage you, and lift you up. Don't give precious mental real estate over to distorted memories of individuals who have the power to bring you down.

TAPPING INTO THE POWER OF FORGIVENESS

Do you have a grievance story that is keeping you chained to a hurtful past? Most of us do.

5. Now consider the hold your grievance story may have on you by asking yourself several questions:

Do you think more about your grievance
story than you do about the good
things that happen in your life? **Yes** **No**

Are you unable to stop thinking about this
event even when you recognize that it is
getting you down? **Yes** **No**

When you think about this hurtful event,
do you find yourself becoming either
physically or emotionally ill? **Yes** **No**

When you tell the story of this event, is
the person who harmed you the central
figure who holds all the power? **Yes** **No**

Do you repeat your grievance story over
and over again without gaining any new
insights? **Yes** **No**

Do you find yourself repeating your story
over and over again to yourself as well as
to others? **Yes** **No**

When you refuse to forgive, you are in effect handcuffing yourself to the person who offended you, to a person you don't even like. And you know the worst thing about that? While you wait for him or her to unlock the cuffs, you are holding the key in your own hand.

Have all your friends already heard this story more than once—and can you tell from their pained expressions that they really don't want to hear it again?   **Yes   No**

Do you feel stuck right where you are in your life, like a victim who has no apparent way out?   **Yes   No**

Do you focus more on your pain than on possible solutions?   **Yes   No**

Is this story limiting your future and the options you have to choose from to achieve what you desire in life?   **Yes   No**

Has the story stayed exactly the same over time, offering no new insights?   **Yes   No**

Do you go down the same well-worn path of thoughts and feelings each time you tell it?   **Yes   No**

If you can answer yes to any of these questions, then you have an old grievance story that is robbing you of energy and keeping you from moving on with your life.

6. When you think about this painful event from your past, how does it affect your life *right now*?

Physically:

- Higher blood pressure

- Stomach ulcers

- Arthritic pain

- Chronic fatigue

- Other: _____

Mentally:

- Anger

- Depression

- Apathy

- Withdrawal

- Other: _____

Spiritually:

- "Life just isn't worth the pain."

- "Who cares?"

- "Do I have any meaningful future to look forward to?"

- "Is there really a God?"

- Other: _____

The frequent retelling of your grievance story may feel empowering—it somehow helps you get even with the one who hurt you—but it actually does nothing except keep you trapped in a painful past. Retelling your grievance story keeps you from imagining new possibilities and taking crucial steps toward achieving the future you really want.

Once you conclude that it's time to let go of your grievance story, forgiveness is the way to do exactly that. Specifically, forgiveness gives you the strength and insight you need to revise your story in the direction of truth and health.

Furthermore, when you forgive the offender, you stop demanding that the past be different, that somehow it must change. The past *never* changes, but how you view

Forgiveness does not suspend the law of cause and effect. What changes is your desire for vengeance and retaliation, and that change helps you avoid an escalation of attacks and counterattacks. Forgiveness frees you.

it can change dramatically. More importantly, how you see the past—whether as a predictor of your future or simply a record of what happened—can make all the difference in the world with how you approach life. No longer does your past define your future. As you extend forgiveness and find freedom from the past, your heart's desires can shape your future. In short, by extending forgiveness, you take back control of your life. Furthermore, your journey toward forgiveness will be helped along when you complete the following two exercises.

Here's the bottom line: your grievance story—more than the person who hurt you—is the enemy responsible for defeating you. And your story defeats you by constantly feeding you a collection of distortions that it passes off as the truth.

7. *Evaluate the incident more carefully.* Your grievance story looks at the painful incident through a very narrow lens. It reports only the elements of the story that make the offender into a villain and you into an innocent victim. Get involved in the healthy process of revising your grievance story by answering the following questions—and be brutally honest! But don't ask yourself the first pair of questions to blame yourself for what the other did to you. Instead, assess what you might do differently to avoid placing yourself in the hurtful situation.

What part did you play in the incident? Put differently, in what way(s) might you have contributed to what happened?

What outside pressures might have prompted the offender to act as he or she did?

What role might his/her background have played in those hurtful actions?

Describe the incident from an outsider's perspective.

What good can you see in the offender?

What good do others see in that person?

In what ways does the incident look different when you put yourself in the offender's shoes?

8. *Act. Don't react.* Actors control how they respond to events, but reactors melt down. So before you react to a hurtful situation or to a memory of that situation, try to calm yourself down. Take some time to choose your response. During those quieter moments, put yourself—as much as you can—somewhere outside of your own skin and try to respond to what happened to you as you imagine an impartial third party might. This exercise reinforces the truth that, as a human being, you can choose your responses to situations. You are not at the whim of emotions, circumstances, or anything else. So learn to act rather than react.

9. What can you do differently to act, rather than react, when others do and say things that hurt you?

REVISITING JILL'S PROBLEM

While there is no question that Tom's irresponsible and selfish actions deeply hurt Jill, there is also no question that her ten years of telling and retelling her sad story have done nothing but keep her resentful, bitter, and chained to a painful past. She may have been telling the story to anyone who would listen in order to either elicit sympathy for her plight or try to punish Tom (by hoping to ruin his reputation, for instance, so that no one will think of him as a good guy). Chances are, however, that he moved on long ago. Jill's anger and her stabs at vengeance hurt no one but herself and her family.

There are lots of people who mistake their imagination for their memory.

— *Josh Billings*

10. If Jill were your best friend, what advice would you offer her in this situation?

11. Jill is focused on how bad Tom is—but at one point she did marry him. What can Jill learn from the reality that her needs blinded her to some of the early warning signals her parents saw?

12. Who is being hurt more by keeping this grievance story alive—Jill or Tom? Explain your answer.

13. Would you coach Jill to spend the majority of her time thinking about what Tom did or to spend time with friends who can build her up? Explain your choice.

14. If you know a Jill, what consequences have you noticed in her life that are an unhealthy byproduct of her grievance story? Consider the following areas:

- Poor health

- Negative attitude

- Fewer friends

- Loss of hope for the future

It was one of those perfect English autumnal days which occur more frequently in memory than in life.

— P. D. James

15. In what way does a grievance story handcuff you, the teller, to a person you don't even like?

16. With all the negative consequences of holding on to a grievance story, why do people still do that?

Jerry and Jim had been best of friends all through high school and college. When they graduated, Jim took a job on the other side of the country. Although they remained friends, they contacted each other less frequently as their lives got busier and their respective careers took off. But whenever they did talk to each other, they immediately recalled all their old experiences and laughed and acted as if they had never been apart.

About five years after graduation, Jerry found out that Jim had married—and had left him off the invitation list. It felt bad enough to Jerry that Jim had not asked Jerry to be in his wedding . . . but not even to be invited? The very thought infuriated Jerry. How could his best friend just ignore him like that?

Jerry vowed that he would never again speak to Jim. Every time he saw a young couple, he thought of his former best friend and just boiled over inside. Eventually Jerry became very explosive, and even his new friends started avoiding him.

When a third party invited Jerry to consider the option of forgiveness, he rejected it out of hand. He believed he could not forgive even if he wanted to. How could Jerry ever forgive Jim for what he had done? And how could he ever let go of his anger?

What You Need to Know

Too often we hurt more than is necessary simply because we would rather suffer than forgive. For some reason we believe that staying angry is better than getting over our anger. Anger, designed to be a fleeting mechanism that helps us deal with an immediate situation, too often grows into a resentment that never gets turned off. (In the book *Forgive to Live* I demonstrate how resentment is the most destructive form of anger.)

Some of us have trouble forgiving because we have a faulty understanding of what forgiveness is. To overcome this barrier, we should first have a clear understanding of what forgiveness is *not*:

Forgiveness means that even though you are wounded, you choose to hurt and suffer less.

— *Fred Luskin*

- *Forgive and forget*. To truly forgive someone does not mean you forget that the hurtful incident ever happened. Some people mistakenly believe they can never forgive because they know they will never be able to forget the wrong done to them. But forgiveness is not forgetfulness! You can remember exactly how someone injured you but still forgive the person from your heart. Through the eyes of forgiveness you will remember, but you will remember the story in a different way.

- *Forgive to make the wrong right*. Forgiveness does not make a wrong into a right any more than a generous tip at a restaurant makes a foul-tasting dinner wonderfully delicious. Forgiveness does not change the past, but it does allow you to make the most of the present and plan for a bright future.

- *Forgive and make up.* Not all forgiveness ends in reconciliation. Sometimes it is not possible—if the other party has died, for example, or is unwilling to reconcile. While it takes two to reconcile, it takes only one to forgive.

Forgiveness is giving up my right to hurt you for hurting me.

—Unknown

- *Forgive and set free.* Forgiveness does not necessarily mean granting a pardon or releasing the guilty party from all the consequences of a hurtful act. The victim of a brutal crime might forgive the felon convicted of the act, for example, but the offender would still have to serve time in jail. Forgiveness does, however, always set free the one who forgives.

1. Which of these four faulty perspectives on forgiveness have you believed at one time or another?

 How has your understanding of forgiveness changed now that you understand these faulty definitions of forgiveness? Be specific.

So what is genuine forgiveness? As you saw at the beginning of the workbook, this is the definition I use:

> *Forgiveness is the process of reframing one's anger and hurt from the past, with the goal of recovering one's peace in the present and revitalizing one's purpose and hopes for the future.*

And as I pointed out earlier, this definition embraces the past, the present, and the future. Genuine forgiveness enables you to come to grips with your past in order to enjoy the present and set sail for a delightful future.

Let me also mention that this workbook focuses on a specific dimension of forgiveness called *personal* forgiveness. Personal forgiveness concentrates on what you need to do with a hurtful incident from your past in order to move beyond it, embrace a present that is peaceful, and pursue a future full of hope and possibilities.

He who cannot forgive others breaks the bridge over which he himself must travel.

— George Herbert

There are other, equally important dimensions of forgiveness that are not developed in this workbook. *Relational* forgiveness, for instance, concerns the dynamics of reconciliation with an estranged friend or family member, while *spiritual* forgiveness deals with repairing one's relationship with God. Although both are important, they lie beyond the scope of this workbook. I have chosen to focus on the personal aspect of forgiveness because it is the area over which you have the most control and from which you can derive the most immediate benefits.

It is also important to understand that genuine forgiveness does not obligate you to return to an old relationship. This is true because:

- *You cannot always restore broken relationships.* While reconciliation might usually seem optimal, it is not always possible. It takes two to make reconciliation happen; you cannot achieve it on your own.

Forgiveness can almost be considered a selfish act because of all the benefits received by the one who forgives.

— Unknown

- *Continuing an abusive relationship could be dangerous.* Forgiveness does not insist that you continue to place yourself in a position to be harmed repeatedly.

- *A forced return to an old relationship often produces bitterness and resentment*, which prevents real forgiveness from taking place.

Personal forgiveness is an effective and practical way of dealing with life's hurts rather than being overwhelmed by them. It is a learned skill that you can master—but it is also a skill that you must consciously choose to develop and use. No one forgives by accident; it takes a deliberate choice to forgive. On the flip side, not to forgive is also a choice.

To forgive or not to forgive: that is the question.

2. Why is it necessary for us to choose to forgive? Why do you think forgiveness doesn't happen naturally?

TAPPING INTO THE POWER OF FORGIVENESS

To be human implies that you have the power of choice. You don't have to behave in a predetermined way merely because someone hurt you. A dog may be ruled by the dictates of stimulus/response, but as a human being, you can choose to pause between the stimulus (the hurt you suffered) and your response and then use that moment to reflect and choose how you will react.

It's choice—not chance—that determines your destiny.

— *Jean Nidetch*

3. To help yourself make the healing choice to forgive, ask yourself some questions.

What do I want my future to look like?

Is prolonged anger or resentment likely to get me to that future?

What are the benefits and/or dangers of prolonged resentment?

What kind of response to the hurt I suffered is most likely to help me attain my goal?

What kind of response is most likely to push it further away?

What specific actions do I need to take *right now* to move me closer to my goals for the future?

If I desire peace in the present and hope for the future, will retelling my grievance story move me in that direction? Why or why not—and if not, what will?

If my anger overwhelms me and I explode, what might the consequences be?

If I continue to harbor resentment, what impact might that have on my future?

Is focusing on this hurtful experience worth sacrificing my peace of mind? If not, then why do people do it?

How much space will I set aside in my mind for this person I don't even like?

Am I so deeply connected to my life goals that this incident will not become a detour or distraction? Explain your answer.

Forgiveness is always a better and therefore a healthier choice than a flat refusal to forgive, but you should not forgive until you feel ready to do so. Don't allow anyone to force you into forgiving. Mandatory forgiveness just is not the genuine article, and it almost always ends up creating more resentment.

One ship sails East, And another West, By the self-same winds that blow, 'Tis the set of the sails, and not the gales, That tells the way we go.

— Ella Wheeler Wilcox

4. To help you ponder whether this is the right time for you to forgive, ask yourself this second set of questions.

   Do I feel pressured or manipulated into offering forgiveness, or am I making a free choice to forgive?

   Am I offering forgiveness because I feel guilty for not forgiving, or because I really want to let go of my hurtful past?

If I do not feel ready to forgive at this time, what do I think is holding me back?

If I do not feel ready to forgive at this time, what do I think needs to happen before I will be ready?

Is my suffering worth holding on to? If not, is it time for me to forgive?

What we call the secret of happiness is no more a secret than our willingness to choose life.

— Leo Buscaglia

Even if you don't feel ready to forgive at this time, be sure to keep forgiveness on your list of options for the future. If you do not keep forgiveness on your list of options, you will never forgive.

5. Remember, forgiveness is a choice. To make it more likely that this is a choice you will make, ponder a third set of questions.

Have I included forgiveness on my list of options for the future?

If forgiveness is not on my list of options, why isn't it?

What will it take for me to choose forgiveness at some point in the future?

What can I do to move forgiveness higher up on my list of options?

When relief from the pain becomes more desirable than holding on to the pain, you are ready to forgive. After all, forgiveness insists that bad things don't have to ruin your today even if they have ruined your yesterdays. Yes, you may have been wronged. Yes, you may feel injured and violated. Forgiveness will change none of that. In fact, any movement toward forgiveness recognizes that we all have to deal with pain in one way or another. Just know that you are not alone on your journey even if your pain is far more visible to you than the pain others suffer.

Your choices are shaped not so much by the event itself, but by your interpretation of that event.

Yes, everyone else on the planet deals with pain in life, just as you do. Whether you will live as a *victim* or a *victor* in response to that pain most often comes down to your conscious choice. Refusing to forgive—or refusing even to place forgiveness on your list of options—almost guarantees that you will remain a victim. Only forgiveness has the power to release you from a painful past. Without forgiveness you will almost certainly remain chained to a person you don't even like. Prolonged anger and bitterness keep you locked up as a prisoner in your mind, but forgiveness serves as the key to release you from your dark cell.

The question is, what will you choose?

REVISITING JERRY'S STORY

Jerry could not see forgiving Jim as a viable option. Jerry believed that the depth of his pain had forever removed forgiveness from his list of options. But what if Jerry had looked more deeply into his grievance story? What new insights might he have uncovered?

You have only one thing to consider when you hit the fork in the road where you must decide between forgiveness and unforgiveness: which is the better choice for you?

For one thing, Jerry might realize that he and Jim had not seen each other for almost five years. Yes, they had talked by phone, but there had been no face-to-face contact in half a decade. Or Jerry could learn that Jim's bride wanted a small wedding with just family and local friends. Since she did not want a large wedding, many genuine friends who were not living near Jim did not receive invitations.

Furthermore, would Jerry have grown quite so angry had he realized that he had done many things in the preceding five years without including or even informing Jerry? He bought his first home during that time, for example, yet never mentioned it to Jim. He had developed a serious relationship, yet Jim never even knew the woman's name. Could Jerry see himself marrying and not inviting Jim? No doubt, under the right set of circumstances, that could have happened.

Finally, Jerry needed to realize that Jim had not suddenly become an evil person. In fact, Jim still had a lot in common with Jerry. So why should Jerry let this one event completely change how he saw Jim?

6. How might all-or-nothing thinking be affecting Jerry's view of Jim?

7. In what ways might a more realistic view that both good and bad things happen in life change Jerry's grievance story about Jim? Be specific.

8. Why might Jerry believe he can't even call Jim and talk about this incident?

9. What would be some advantages and disadvantages to calling Jim? List them below.

10. While Jerry believes he has no choice but to avoid Jim, what alternative choices do you see?

11. Jerry may not be ready to forgive Jim right now, but what could Jerry do that might make forgiveness a more likely option in the future? Be specific.

*S*ally tried to be the perfect wife. She would have supper ready, keep the house clean, and set aside all of her interests just to be with Jeff. But it seemed as if nothing she did was good enough. Jeff ignored her, and the two of them seemed to live in separate worlds.

One day when Sally returned earlier than expected from visiting her mother, she found another woman in her home with Jeff. Furious, Sally kicked her cheating husband out of the house.

But Sally had no idea how to deal with her loss in healthy ways. For years her life revolved around that terrible evening and what Jeff had put her through. So, rather than moving on with her life, she took every opportunity to tell all her friends what a terrible person Jeff was—that is, the few friends she had left. People who knew Sally tried to avoid her and her bitterness as if she were wearing a necklace of the most potent garlic. And the temporary satisfaction Sally obtained from talking about no-good Jeff provided very little relief from the misery of her wounded existence.

Meanwhile, Jeff had gone on with his life, remarried, and of course had no interest in staying in touch with Sally. This further infuriated Sally, so she would occasionally send Jeff a letter letting him (and anyone else who might read the letter) know what a terrible man he was. After a time, the letters started coming back with the notation "Return to sender. Addressee unknown."

Tragically, Sally remained imprisoned by her anger and totally unaware that she was choosing to remain trapped by her miserable story.

WHAT YOU NEED TO KNOW

Celebrated author John Updike once said, "In memory's telephoto lens, far objects are magnified." His words accurately describe what tends to happen in the human mind. Events we remember often become distorted over time—some details are indeed magnified, but others are overlooked—so that our memories offer only a partially accurate picture of what actually happened.

Specifically, our grievance stories feature only certain aspects of past events, always magnifying the evil of the offender and focusing on the events that reinforce our grievance. These stories keep us trapped in a painful past by highlighting the worst elements of our experience and keeping our attention locked on the most hurtful parts of our story. To gain further insight into how this works, please refer to chapter 5 in the book *Forgive to Live*.

It's always easier to see a problem in someone else than it is to see problems in ourselves. But until you can see both sides of the problem, you can't see the real problem.

Acknowledging the existence of your painful past and the fact that you can't change it is a key step toward forgiveness. Forgiveness then goes on to insist that you can most definitely change your memory of the painful event. And by insisting that you adjust your inaccurate memories, forgiveness gives you the power to get unstuck from your past.

The process of adjusting these faulty memories is called "reframing." When you reframe your grievance story, you look at it from a different and bigger-picture perspective. Placing your experience in a larger context will help you recall the offense more accurately, and that makes the story less hurtful.

To better understand this reframing concept, imagine the picture frame around a painting or photograph. The dimensions of the chosen frame will focus your eye by purposefully including or excluding certain parts of the picture. The smaller the frame, the less of the picture you see and the narrower the story it tells. Likewise, all of our grievance stories choose a very small frame that yields a very limited and therefore skewed perspective.

If your frame is small and only bad stuff appears within it, then it's easy to conclude that your whole life is ruined, for nothing good appears in the story to offset the pain. Misery is all you see in your life. But if you choose a larger frame that includes both good and bad elements, you make room in your life for hope. The larger your frame—the bigger your perspective—the less any single event can derail your life.

When you choose forgiveness—when you work to reframe your grievance story with a larger and therefore healthier perspective—you are saying, "I'm not going to

People who refuse to stop focusing on the hurtful behavior of others—who will not take responsibility for their own happiness—end up discouraged, unhappy, and usually alone.

Our friends are those who know their own faults well enough to forgive ours.

— Moulton Farnham

Forgiveness is the way to work through your problems rather than to walk around them. Forgiveness heals the hurt rather than hiding it.

hold a grievance any longer. I'm not going to keep stoking my anger. I'm not going to continue to ponder my right to vengeance and my plans for revenge. I'm going to let all that go."

And "letting go" means letting go of your old grievance story and replacing it with a new, more accurate story. Letting go does not mean you forget what happened. It simply means that you retell the story in a different way; you, in effect, make it a different story. You don't lie to yourself; you don't pretend that the event wasn't really important or didn't really hurt. But reframing your story by placing it in a better perspective will take away its power over your life. By making it more accurate you will make it less able to continue hurting you.

1. Explain why people would use the smallest frame possible to construct their grievance story.

2. Why does using a larger frame lead to a more accurate recall of the past?

As you begin the process of reframing your grievance story, keep in mind three crucial truths that underlie the possibility of forgiveness:

- You cannot change the past.

- You cannot change the person who hurt you.

- You cannot make life fair.

Do not judge, or you too will be judged.

— Jesus Christ

If you want to find peace for today and hope for tomorrow, you have little choice but to reframe the grievance story that is keeping you trapped in the past and hurting you in the present. Fortunately, when you exercise the power of forgiveness, both peace and hope are well within your grasp.

TAPPING INTO THE POWER OF FORGIVENESS

Below are the six primary steps involved in reframing a grievance story and so changing a painful memory. Each step is important, and is best tackled in the order given below.

*I. Focus on what's true from **both** points of view.*

You have a particular perspective on the painful incident that prompted your grievance story, but so does the person in your story whom you consider the offender! Rarely is one party completely at fault and the other totally to blame. Part of reframing asks you to look for truth from all relevant points of view.

3. Answering the following questions will help you see your story from other perspectives.

What true observations from the other person's point of view can I add to my picture of what happened?

What important details do I consistently leave out of my story?

In what specific ways would the other person's account of this incident differ from my own?

In what specific ways might my own actions have contributed to what happened?

Two key characteristics make forgiveness more likely to occur: they are humility and empathy.

II. Develop empathy for the person who hurt you.

Try to see the other person as a real human being, not as a demon who is completely and irredeemably evil. To empathize means that you try to understand what might have motivated the behavior you found so hurtful.

4. Answering the questions can help you develop empathy for the person who hurt you:

   What do I know about the other person's background that might help to explain what he/she did?

   What circumstances in his/her life at the time of the incident might help to explain that hurtful action?

What kind of pressures was the person who hurt me dealing with?

How might he/she have interpreted my actions leading up to the hurtful event?

What do other people think of this person?

If this hurtful event had never occurred, what opinion of this person might I hold?

Humility not only allows you to see others as equal to yourself, but it also requires you to see yourself as equal to others. This awareness actually paves the way for forgiveness to take place.

III. *Identify the wrongs you yourself have committed that need to be forgiven.*

All of us need forgiveness, and that includes you. Once you realize that you have done things that require forgiveness and that you have received the forgiveness you needed, you will most likely be much more open to forgiving the person who hurt you. When you develop an attitude of humility—"There but for the grace of God go I"—you find it much easier to forgive people who hurt you.

5. Be totally honest as you answer these questions that encourage an attitude of humility.

   What offenses have I committed that I consider completely out of character for me?

What mistakes have I made that hurt others? Who has graciously forgiven me for the wrongs I've committed?

Have I ever asked someone for forgiveness, and not received it? If so, how did that make me feel?

Why should I consider myself any more worthy of forgiveness than the person who hurt me?

As you look at the hurtful event more carefully, what role might you have played in what happened?

IV. *Revise your story so that it more accurately reflects reality.*

Take some time now to dissect your original grievance story. Identify the elements of your story that need a small frame in order to appear true. Then make your frame as large as you can and try to see the hurtful incident as one small part of a bigger picture. Your goal is to make your story more comprehensive and therefore more accurate.

6. To give your story a bigger frame, answer these questions:

From whose perspective can I look at the hurtful event in order to increase the size of my frame?

What elements of the full picture have I so far excluded from my story?

What might be keeping me from enlarging my frame?

What is the largest frame for my story that I can imagine?

When a humble person looks in the mirror, he or she recognizes the absurdity of saying that someone is unworthy or undeserving of forgiveness.

V. Imagine your desired outcome and make adjustments toward that end.

Forgiveness looks ahead as well as behind. In looking ahead, it frees you to picture the kind of future that will bring you the greatest amount of satisfaction and fulfillment. Forgiveness releases you from the shackles of a painful past so that you can take specific, appropriate steps toward achieving the future you desire.

7. Answer these questions to determine if you're ready to move toward that future:

    What from my past do I need to start letting go of?

    What can I start doing today to put to rest an inaccurate version of my past that only keeps me in chains?

    What kind of future do I want for myself? Be specific.

What specific actions can I start doing *today* to help my desired future become a reality?

VI. Realize that forgiveness takes time; it is almost never a one-time event.

Like most things in life, forgiveness takes practice. Rarely can someone in a single instant forgive so completely and comprehensively that those old, negative thoughts never resurface. It may take awhile for you to "let go" and thus experience all the tremendous benefits of forgiveness. It takes practice—so start practicing today.

Understanding is not the same as condoning the hurtful act or granting permission to do it again. Understanding through empathy does not make the action right, but empathy does give you a different perspective on the person's limitations.

8. Answering these questions will help you along your journey of forgiveness:

Have I begun to use and practice the principles of forgiveness I've learned so far? If so, what difference is it making in my life? If I haven't, why not?

When I hit a roadblock to forgiveness, how do I usually respond? If I don't like my normal response, what can I do differently the next time around?

What can I tell myself to grant myself grace and be more patient with myself as I practice forgiveness?

REVISITING SALLY'S STORY

With the help of a class on forgiveness, Sally eventually recognized that her consistent focus on the hurtful behavior of her ex-husband injured only herself. In fact, the only life she was destroying was her own.

Sally realized that she could continue to believe that her life was miserable because Jeff had made it that way, or she could let that old story go and find happiness in the new and healthier life made possible by forgiveness.

Humility and empathy pave the way for forgiveness. As they work together to lower your resistance to forgiveness, humility and empathy actually make forgiveness more likely to occur.

9. Which of the following unalterable truths might Sally have been trying to change?

   • You cannot change the past.

   • You cannot change the other person.

   • You cannot make life fair.

   How might accepting these truths make it easier for Sally to move on?

10. Although Jeff and Sally are different people, they did not come from totally different worlds. If Sally recalled things she and Jeff had in common, how might her view of him change?

Forgiveness doesn't change the reality of the past, but it does have the power to change your memory of the past. When you reframe your grievance story, you take much of the sting out of your past and transfer control of your life back into your own hands.

11. Neither Sally nor Jeff is perfect, and that means she can learn from her marriage and divorce. What lessons inherent in the heartbreak might help her avoid repeating old mistakes?

12. In what way(s) might Sally reframe her old story about her marriage to Jeff in order to release herself from being the victim?

13. What options for improving her situation does Sally have *today*?

14. Why would her ability to forgive Jeff help Sally release herself from the past and move into a happier future?

15. Why can forgiving someone sometimes feel as if you're letting that person off the hook? Who really gets let off the hook when you forgive? Explain.

*M*ark had a very domineering father who wanted Mark to follow in his footsteps and pursue a medical career like he had. When Mark showed other interests, his father did everything he could to keep his son from pursuing them, including refusing to help with any college expenses. Mark eventually buckled under the pressure and chose to pursue a career in medicine.

Mark spent the next eight years of his life doing a job he hated—all the while nurturing deep resentment toward his dad. Mark's rising blood pressure forced him to start taking medications. Since his dad also had high blood pressure, Mark chalked his condition up to heredity. It never occurred to him that he had developed high blood pressure at a much younger age than his dad.

Mark finally realized that living the life his father wanted for him, rather than the one he desired, was ruining his life. After participating in a course on forgiveness, Mark also recognized that his resentment toward his father had contributed significantly to his high blood pressure. So Mark made the decision to forgive his dad.

At long last Mark felt free to pursue his true interests. He was older now, and he had saved enough money that he could afford to work in the area of his real passion. So Mark took up gardening, and soon his flowering plant business was thriving. Mark not only took time to smell the roses: he also cut, trimmed, and sold roses. Mark thoroughly enjoyed his new career. "It was such a relief to release my anger toward my dad," Mark said.

Mark also learned to relax and not push so hard in life. He especially benefited by taking short time-outs throughout the day. He'd simply take several deep breaths and relax his whole body. This practice, along with his work on forgiveness, helped him to get off his blood-pressure medications.

Mark's friends noticed the change in him. He was not as short tempered as he had been. He experienced a peace he had never before known.

What You Need to Know

Forgiveness is giving up all hope for a better past. The truth is that you will never find contentment by obsessing about the past or wishing you could change it. You can impact only the here and now. Contentment blossoms when what you have (the present) overshadows concerns about what you lack (the past) and worries about what you want (the future).

But sometimes we have a problem getting to or staying in that place of contentment. We've tried reframing our grievance story, but the pain is just too fresh and too raw for us to complete the task. Or perhaps we've finished our reframing exercise, but at times the old feelings emerge without warning. What can we do then?

Since a peaceful state of mind gives you a better vantage point for tackling the challenges of life, you need to find a way to experience some peace in the present, a respite from the conflict. Fortunately, you can choose from two routes to that soothing destination, and both work equally well. You will find a fuller description of what follows in chapter 9 of the book *Forgive to Live*.

Because your mind and your body are intimately and inseparably connected, your thoughts and feelings affect your body's physiological response, just as a change in your body's physiological activity alters your thoughts and feelings. The process works in both directions:

THOUGHT ⇒ FEELING ⇒ PHYSIOLOGICAL RESPONSE

PHYSIOLOGICAL CHANGE ⇒ FEELING ⇒ THOUGHT

In other words, if you feel upset about some hurtful event from the past, you can alter those feelings and find some peace either by changing your thoughts or relaxing your body.

First, consider changing your thoughts. Contrary to what many people assume, you don't have to allow unpleasant thoughts to continue to assault you. You don't have to think about whatever happens to pop into your head. If the default channel in your mind keeps replaying the old story of how you've been unfairly hurt, then change the channel. Choose to think about something else. Don't try to stop thinking about the unpleasant event; that won't work. Instead, make the conscious decision to start thinking about something else.

The greatest discovery of my generation is that a human being can alter his life by altering his attitude.

— William James

Some people have found it very effective to carry around a small clicker that sounds like a remote control changing the channel on the TV. When they find themselves thinking about an issue they'd rather not ponder at that moment, they reach into their pocket, click the clicker, and start thinking about something else—maybe what they want for dinner that night, where they want to go on their next vacation, or how much they enjoyed their last visit with an old friend. The point is, by altering their thoughts—changing the channel—they inevitably modify their feelings and so change their physiological response. As a result they experience a measure of peace instead of turmoil.

You can observe a lot by just watching.

— Yogi Berra

The other route, that is equally as helpful, involves changing the body's activity in order to make room for calmer thoughts. One effective method is called diaphragmatic breathing. By taking controlled, deep, leisurely breaths, you slow your body's rhythms, your thoughts slow down and more peaceful feelings begin to take over. Diaphragmatic breathing relaxes the body, quiets the mind, and places you in the here and now rather than in some troubling moment from the past or some imagined difficulty in the future.

Another technique that moves you to the same place of calm is called progressive muscle relaxation. In this exercise you tighten and relax various muscle groups in a predetermined sequence (described in "Tapping into the Power of Forgiveness" on page 91), thus bringing a measure of peace to both body and soul. You can maxi-

Focusing on the present places you in a position where you can be in control—and the truth is, you can only control what happens in the here and now.

mize the benefits of both these exercises by doing them for two to three minutes, five to eight times a day.

While the preceding exercises can help you to alter your thoughts and feelings by using internal mechanisms, you can also alter your external environment and achieve similar results. Four external factors in particular will help you experience more peace in the present.

- *Light* can have a profound impact on how upbeat or downcast you feel. In general, the more natural light you have, the better off you will be.

- *Color* also contributes to your sense of peace. In general, earth tones have a calming effect, while bright, intense hues tend to create more tension.

- *Aromas* can have a powerful effect, although various smells trigger highly individualized responses. Lilacs, for example, may remind one person of delightful days in the countryside, but instantly put someone else in the dentist's office.

- *Sound* can also prompt highly individualized responses, but, in general, stress is caused by a heavy beat and major dissonance, while a soft melody and gentler tones usually encourage calmness.

TAPPING INTO THE POWER OF FORGIVENESS

Do a mental review of your last few days. Have you noticed any physical symptoms from the stress and anger you might have experienced because of unresolved issues with your grievance story? If so, you may benefit from practicing one or more of the techniques mentioned above and discussed in greater detail below.

1. First, though, explain why experiencing peace in the present can help you forgive.

CHANGE YOUR THOUGHTS.

Picture in your mind a fresh-picked lemon. See the dimples in its yellow skin? Slice it and squeeze some juice into your mouth. Let it drop on your tongue and taste its tartness. Feel the saliva fill your mouth. You have to swallow, don't you? Sure you do—and the stronger the image of a lemon is in your mind, the more saliva your body will produce. Got the picture? Good!

You can change what you feel and therefore how your body reacts by choosing to think about something else.

It is probably no happenstance that, in many world languages, the word for spirit is the same word that is used for breath. RUACH is Hebrew for both spirit and breath. PNEUMA is Greek for both spirit and breath. SPIRITUS is Latin for both spirit and breath. CHI is Japanese for both spirit and breath.

Now stop thinking about the lemon. I told you to stop thinking about the lemon. You're still thinking about that lemon, aren't you? The harder you try to stop thinking about the lemon, the more you think about that lemon. I'm going to try something else.

A little background. I come from New England, where my favorite fruit—especially in the fall—is a crisp Vermont Gold apple. Nothing can compare to an apple fresh off the tree. As soon as you get past its unique gold and red skin, the apple becomes snowy white, and the sweet juicy inside is just to die for. And there is nothing like the distinct crunch of an apple picked right from the tree on a brisk autumn day.

Did you notice what just happened? For the last fifteen seconds, you weren't thinking about a lemon; you were focusing on the apple. Why? Because you changed your mental channel. By choosing to think about a second thing (apples), you stopped thinking about the first thing (lemons).

You just demonstrated that it really is possible to change your thoughts. And by choosing your thoughts, you also choose your emotional response. Feeling follows thought. So, if you don't like what is currently playing in your mind—if it makes you angry and bitter—then change the channel. Like using the remote control of your TV, you can change the channel in your mind any time you so choose.

2. Think about changing the channel of your thoughts. What is your own internal default channel? What do you find yourself thinking about when nothing else needs your attention?

3. Describe what you can do to change the channel when you don't want those thoughts playing in  your mind.

TRY DIAPHRAGMATIC BREATHING.

- Get in a comfortable position either sitting in a chair or lying on the floor. Be careful not to slouch because that can restrict your breathing. Don't be stiff, but keep your spine as straight as you comfortably can.

- As you slowly inhale, think of your belly as a balloon. Place your hands on your belly as it expands and contracts. Watch your hands rise as you inhale and fall each time you exhale.

All of life consists of cycles of stress and recovery. Tension depletes energy, but relaxation releases tension and gives you more energy to invest in life.

- Fill your lungs and then empty them completely. You may want to push gently on your belly each time you exhale to ensure that you are emptying your lungs. As you slowly inhale and exhale, your heart rate and blood pressure will start to go down. As you slow down, your tensed muscles will also start to relax. They do so because you are soothing every muscle in your body with rich, oxygenated blood, enabling them to relax and rebuild.

- Breathe slowly. For a good pace, slowly count to five as you inhale; then count to five as you exhale. Pause briefly in the moment between exhaling and inhaling.

- Breathe in through your nose and out through your mouth. Doing so allows a slight cooling of the nasal passage and can actually cool your brain. A cool thinker really does make better decisions than a hot-head, so chill.

4. What happens to your thoughts and feelings when you breathe like this?

5. Are you ready to start taking several breathing breaks during the course of your day? Why or why not?

TRY PROGRESSIVE MUSCLE RELAXATION.

A. Begin with the breathing exercise just described.

With practice, you will become proficient at calming your body and quieting your mind, thus equipping yourself to move forward with the crucial work of forgiveness.

B. Every time you inhale, tighten a muscle group. Every time you exhale, release and relax the muscles you just tightened. Let your muscles go totally limp and pause for a second or two before inhaling again. I suggest moving through the muscle groups in the following order:

- Your toes
- The arches in your feet
- Your calf muscles
- Your thighs
- Your buttocks
- Your stomach
- Your chest
- Your hands (make a fist)
- Your forearms
- Your biceps
- Your shoulders
- Your neck
- Your jaw and your temples

C. Tighten and relax each muscle group three times before moving on to the next.

D. If you notice particular tension in any muscle group, exercise those muscles five times.

As you do this exercise, you're letting go not only of your stress, but also of the high-energy emotions that cause your stress. You simply cannot sustain intense thoughts or feelings when you're physically relaxed.

6. What happens to your thoughts and feelings when you relax your muscles like this?

7. Are you ready to start making time throughout the day to relax like this? Why or why not?

8. Once you have learned to experience a measure of peace, identify something you wanted to do in life but were unable to for whatever reason. What decision can you make *today* to do that very thing?

9. Light, colors, aromas, and sound can affect our sense of peace.

   What have you noticed about how light affects your moods? What change can you make in the lighting around you to improve your outlook?

   What colors tend to bring you feelings of peace? What colors tend to make you feel more anxious?

What aromas give you a sense of calm? Which ones make you feel agitated?

What will you do to use sound to help you achieve a more relaxed and peaceful environment at home? At work? In your car?

REVISITING MARK'S STORY

Although Mark's father never apologized for what he did, the two of them got along better once Mark was able to forgive his dad. And now Mark could see how much

Far too many of us make the mistake of trying to live in the past or in the future. The truth is, the only time we are ever alive is now. So do what you must to find peace in the present—and don't forget to enjoy yourself!

his dad loved his work, so it made sense to him why his father truly believed that if Mark would only give it a try, he would love it as well.

As Mark said about this experience, "By giving up the resentment I had toward my dad, I was able to adopt a more mature view of life. I took a larger view of things and could place things in a broader perspective, which helped me to make better decisions. I could now use the energy I once wasted on obsessing about my dad's treatment of me to focus on the goals I most wanted to achieve."

10. Mark's resentment toward his dad was having adverse effects on his physical health. If you feel resentment against someone, what physical symptoms might you be experiencing in part because of that resentment?

11. Changing the channel in your mind can bring immediate relief, but what dangers might there be in us-
ing this technique too frequently?

12. You are a unique individual, so your mind will affect your body in unique ways. Pay attention to
when your body feels better or feels worse. What
were you doing and thinking at the time you felt
better or worse?

 13. Do you consider being still a waste of time? Why or why not?

 14. Explain how stillness and peacefulness can help you do the hard work of forgiveness.

*P*eter didn't think of himself as an angry person. Sure, he could get upset—but only when provoked! But basically he was a nice guy who would give you the shirt off his back.

Peter worked three years at a menial job. Every time he thought of quitting, his boss asked him to stick it out a little longer, reminding Peter that when the company went public, all its employees would be eligible for stock options.

When the time came for his annual raise, Peter was told that the company had to show a profit in order to get top dollar when it went public, so he would not be getting a raise this year. "But don't worry about it," his boss told him, "because the stock options when we go public will be worth far more than a small raise in salary." So Peter stayed at the low-paying job he hated.

Then the day came when the company went public. Everyone in management received thousands of shares in the new company, but Peter and the other frontline workers received only one hundred shares each, amounting to only about $1,000 worth of stock.

Peter complained bitterly to his boss, who replied he could do nothing about the decision. The board of directors claimed that those in upper management should be rewarded the most because they had taken the greatest risks. This explanation did nothing to assuage Peter's anger and bitterness, so his boss fired him on the spot for insubordination.

Peter felt so angry that he thought long and hard about how to get back at the company in some destructive way.

WHAT YOU NEED TO KNOW

When someone has wronged you, most people feel the desire to get revenge. We want life to be fair: "an eye for an eye and a tooth for a tooth." When life isn't fair and there's nothing we can do about it, we get angry.

It is one of the great mysteries of life: all of us know an angry person, but not one of us is an angry person.

Yet many of us have trouble admitting our anger, even when it erupts. Few of us see ourselves as angry, but most of us have no trouble identifying at least one angry person we know. Apparently we find it easy to recognize anger in others, but very difficult to see it in ourselves. Why? Here are three reasons:

- We tend to justify our anger.

- We assume the worst motives for others and the best motives for ourselves.

- We are taught to believe that showing anger is wrong.

Anyone can get angry—that is easy—but to do this to the right person, to the right extent, at the right time, with the right motive, and in the right way, that is not for everyone, nor is it easy.

— Aristotle

Maybe you have trouble admitting your anger—but can you acknowledge that you've been hurt? Probably. So consider this fact: most experts consider anger a secondary response to hurt. We get angry when we are hurt. In other words, anger is a signal alerting us to some hurt we've suffered, even if we can't immediately identify what that hurt might be.

Our anger, therefore, can be a good thing. Its presence indicates that something has gone wrong and lets us know we need to deal with it. Anger also gives us the energy to confront some danger to our health or well-being. It can push us to clarify our real goals and to identify the obstacles that keep us from achieving those goals. Anger enables us to assert ourselves, and the result can be a greater sense of self-worth. Anger can also empower us to find a winning solution to a hurtful problem. And, if harnessed correctly, anger can lead to a spirited and rewarding life.

The fact is, we all get angry. And a necessary step toward practicing forgiveness is to recognize that you have been hurt and that, as a result, you feel angry.

If we don't handle our anger effectively, however, it can cause all sorts of problems. In addition to creating a smorgasbord of serious medical issues, unresolved anger tends to work against our willingness to offer forgiveness and therefore keeps us trapped in an ugly, painful past. (To better see how this works, see chapter 3 in the book *Forgive to Live*.) Sometimes we remain angry because we like the attention it gets us. And some of us like the feeling of power that anger can give us; we have learned to use our anger to intimidate others or make them feel guilty.

So what exactly is the most helpful way to express our anger? Three basic choices exist. We can express our anger:

- *Passively*—as revealed by such behaviors as ignoring, wishing, withdrawing, accommodating, and avoiding

- *Aggressively*—as revealed by such behaviors as attacking, forcing, criticizing, controlling, and harming others

- *Assertively*—as revealed by such behaviors as confronting, being honest, stating expectations, setting boundaries, and detaching

1. Do you most naturally express your anger passively, aggressively, or assertively? Give details from your life that support your answer.

If you want to express your anger most effectively, choose the assertive option. Assertiveness takes responsibility, not necessarily for what happened, but for what will happen in the future. Healthy assertiveness allows you to express to the people around you how you feel and what you expect without attacking them. This approach carries the least risk of escalating the problem. The implication clearly is that one of the best ways to deal with your anger is to express your *hurt*, rather than your *anger*, since people tend to listen to hurt much more readily than they do to anger.

Perhaps most important, dealing with your anger in an assertive way can pave the way for forgiveness, while passive and aggressive responses tend to make forgiveness far less likely. So what does an assertive expression of anger look like? Consider these guidelines for healthy, assertive behavior.

A. Confront the problem when it arises by facing the situation head-on, before it has a chance to fester.

B. State as objectively as you can your point of view and be careful to use "I" statements rather than "you" statements. Say, for example, "I feel like I am not important to you when you come home late without letting me know" instead of "You don't care one bit about me, or you would have called." "I" statements talk about what I need, not about what you must do for me.

C. Make your communication clear and specific. Say, for instance, "It would be helpful if you would call as soon as you know you are going to be late so I can change plans on this end" rather than "What do you think? That the whole world revolves around your schedule?"

D. Assertiveness focuses more on the ways you have been hurt than on how angry you are. This can be helpful because other people can listen much more easily to words that express hurt than to words that express anger. Also, assertiveness seeks to clarify and resolve the problem, not to escalate it.

E. Being assertive means setting clear boundaries. If you say no, then mean it. Don't give in for the sake of peace when you know you will regret it afterwards.

F. Establish consequences when necessary, and this will reinforce that you mean what you say.

Holding on to anger is a lot like holding on to a hot rock. As you clench it tightly in your fist, ready to hurl it at the person who did that awful thing to you, you are in fact hurting only yourself.

All of us get angry because all of us get hurt. But forgiveness means giving up your right to vengeance, in part because it is necessary for the continued existence of society, but also for your own good.

Now, understand that you can give up vengeance without having to give up justice. Vengeance wants to even the score in order to feel the satisfaction of some sort of retribution. Justice, on the other hand, aims to improve an individual's or the community's quality of life by requiring the offender to pay a fair penalty. Justice calls for a specific price to be paid; vengeance never feels satisfied, regardless of the price. Justice is achievable; vengeance never is.

Unresolved anger can lead directly to heart disease and other serious illnesses, but by practicing forgiveness you can reverse its harmful effects.

Back to the core issue of anger. None of us chooses to become angry, but we most certainly choose how we respond to the hurt that triggered our anger. Two primary pathways exist, as described below. How you choose to deal with your anger will put you on either the road to bitter or the road to better.

Bitter	**Better**
You make me angry.	I make myself angry.

Therefore

Your actions caused my feelings and behaviors.	My thoughts and actions determine how I feel and what I do.

Therefore

You must change so I can feel better again.	I choose how I live my life.

Therefore

If you do not change, I will resent you, and I will be miserable for the rest of my life.	I am free to do what I need to do for my well-being. I will go on with my life and live happily ever after.

TAPPING INTO THE POWER OF FORGIVENESS

Sometimes we don't recognize our anger because we don't become red-faced lunatics shouting obscenities at the top of our lungs. But anger varies in intensity and therefore can be much more subtle, as the continuum below illustrates:

Annoyed ⇒ *Irritated* ⇒ **Upset** ⇒ *Hostile* ⇒ **Enraged** ⇒ *Resentful*

Each one of these degrees of intensity falls under the heading of anger. And the most damaging of all—physically, psychologically, and spiritually—is resentment. To better understand how you deal with your anger, write down your responses to the following questions:

  2. On the continuum of anger (above), where do you most often find yourself?

3. In what specific ways does your anger most often reveal itself?

I've had a few arguments with people, but I never carry a grudge. You know why? While you're carrying a grudge, they're out dancing.

— Buddy Hackett

4. How do you tend to deal with your anger when it surfaces? Do you deny that you are angry, mentally prepare your revenge, or react with more anger of your own? Give a recent example.

5. In what ways might your anger be keeping you from offering forgiveness?

Admitting your anger and seeing that it might be connected to some hurt you've suffered are good first steps. But then what are you going to do with your anger? Too often you might feel tempted to choose one of the following seven ineffective strategies for dealing with your anger:

I. *You overlook the hurt and pretend that it didn't really happen.*

In what ways do you sometimes overlook the hurts others cause you?

What happens both inside you and to the relationship when you pretend you're not really hurt?

To carry a grudge is like being stung to death by a single bee.

— *William H. Walton*

II. *You focus on the unfair behavior of the other person.*

What is the difference between acknowledging someone's unfair behavior and focusing on it?

How can you tell when you're focusing in an unhealthy way on someone's unfair behavior? What
are some telltale signs?

III. *You displace your anger on a third party.*

Upon what third party are you most likely to focus your anger?

What makes this third party an inviting target for your anger?

IV. *You deny your anger.*

Under what circumstances are you most likely to deny your anger?

Why are you sometimes tempted to deny your anger?

V. *You develop a mental picture of revenge.*

What kinds of revenge against the one who hurt you have you imagined?

What do you hope this mental picture of revenge will do for you?

VI. *You use drugs, alcohol, or food to numb your pain.*

Are you more likely to use drugs, alcohol, or food to numb your pain?

While you may experience some short-term relief, what is the longer-term price you will pay by coping with your anger this way?

VII. *You become cynical about life.*

Do you consider yourself a cynic? Why or why not?

In what ways does cynicism help you deal with your pain? How effective is the option of cynicism?

If you realize that your hurt over some past incident (or incidents) is making you angry in the present, what can you do to reduce your anger effectively?

6. Start by answering these questions:

In light of everything else that is going on
in my world, is this issue important enough
to invest my energy and time in?   **Yes   No**

Am I truly justified in harboring my
anger?   **Yes   No**

Will remaining angry make a significant difference
in my circumstances? Explain.

What price am I paying by holding on to my anger?

REVISITING PETER'S STORY

Peter was fortunate enough to have a friend who advised him to seek legal counsel before he acted out his fantasies of revenge. "Your former employer didn't have to give you anything," the lawyer told Peter, "since none of the promises were ever put into writing."

These words made Peter even angrier than he had been. But as the conversation continued, the attorney did think that Peter could pursue a case of wrongful discharge, a suit that is currently in court.

Our word RESENT comes from a French term that means "to feel again." Grudges do little to punish the offender, but they do a great job of causing us to repeatedly feel the pain the offender originally caused us.

7. What hurt is fueling Peter's anger? Is Peter's anger at his former employer justified? Why or why not?

8. What would you advise Peter to do with his anger?

9. Is Peter's pursuit of this issue in court consistent with forgiveness? Explain why or why not.

10. What could Peter do to try to remain objective so his anger does not overwhelm him?

11. What does Peter need to do to keep this situation from spawning a grievance story that could ruin his life?

12. When someone hurts you, do you tend to express your hurt or your anger? Why? If you answered "anger," what can you do to train yourself to express your hurt?

*M*aria was living in extreme poverty in Eastern Europe. Todd was an American soldier serving in that country. During his tour of duty there, the two met.

Maria was looking for a way out of poverty, Todd was looking for someone to take care of him, and their mutual needs prompted them to get married. After going through seemingly endless immigration hoops, Todd was finally allowed to bring Maria back to the United States. And that's when the relationship problems began.

Todd suffered from low self-esteem, so to make himself feel better, he made life miserable for Maria. He would not let her work outside the home. He constantly belittled her and treated her like a child instead of his wife. He taught Maria enough English to enable her to understand his orders, but not enough to communicate effectively with others.

When company did visit, he embarrassed her in terrible ways. He made fun of her cooking, ordered her to do every menial task, and then mocked her "stupidity" about the ways of Americans.

Soon Maria developed high blood pressure and a serious case of ulcers, which at times got so bad that she could hardly move. She saw a physician who not only prescribed some medications, but also advised her to make some lifestyle changes: he explained that her anger and resentment would kill her.

Maria considered leaving Todd, but she saw no way to survive if she left him. Besides, every day she ran into reminders that everything she *had in this world was a result of Todd's generosity. And so her resentment grew—resentment about the way Todd treated her, resentment that she was stuck in this situation—and it tore her apart emotionally and further weakened her physical health.*

WHAT YOU NEED TO KNOW

Anger kills. The American Heart Association warns that a person prone to anger is three times more likely to have a heart attack than someone who is not.

Furthermore, Dr. Redford Williams at Duke University has powerfully demonstrated that anger kills. In one study, for instance, he reviewed the anger scores of 225 physicians who had graduated from medical school twenty-five years earlier. When they first began their medical training, each student was required to take a psychological test, part of which measured hostility or anger. Dr. Williams arranged the old anger scores from the highest to the lowest. Then he sent out a questionnaire asking these physicians about their current health.

Dr. Williams discovered that those with the highest anger scores while they were in school also had the highest incidences of heart disease and death twenty-five years later. He used this data to support his theory that one's anger could accurately predict illness, particularly heart disease.

The most common symptoms of living in the world of anger and resentment are elevated blood pressure, chronic headaches, stomach disorders, joint pain, and fatigue. (For a more in-depth discussion of how anger can impair one's health, see chapter 4 in the book *Forgive to Live*.) When you get angry, your body releases adrenalin into your bloodstream, causing your cardiac system to increase your heart rate and thus increasing your blood pressure. That initial response—the increased heart rate, increased blood pressure, change of kidney function, release of fat into the bloodstream, and increased cholesterol in your bloodstream—is not the problem. This sequence of physiological events benefits you when your anger lasts only a short time, enabling you to address the immediate situation.

The problem comes when your anger sticks around for prolonged periods of time. That is when your health is at risk. In fact, people who hold on to their anger are the most stressed individuals that doctors see, and these people suffer the most physical ailments, such as headaches, stomach problems, muscle tension, and high blood pressure.

1. Do you ever find yourself repressing anger? If so, in what ways do you tend to do this—and why?

So what can you do to reduce chronic, prolonged anger? Enter forgiveness. Forgiveness reduces anger and this reality can be verified through the use of standardized anger expression tests. By learning to practice forgiveness, you can:

- Start doing something about a worrisome physical condition

- Move the locus of control from what someone else did in the past to what you can do in the present

- Begin the process of letting go, changing your grievance story, and moving on with your life

- Lower your blood pressure

- Enjoy a spiritual awakening

Forgiveness really is the solution to the trap so many of us fall into, namely, that life isn't fair. In short, *forgiveness has the potential to bring healing to the whole person: body, mind, and spirit.* Forgiving is not a way to avoid pain, but to heal pain. Forgiveness does not excuse bad behavior, but rather bravely deals with it head-on.

You can forgive only if you want to, and you will want to only when you recognize the price you are paying for not forgiving.

As you practice forgiveness over the next several months—or, put differently, whenever you experience anger—note how your body reacts. Pay particularly close attention to:

- Muscle tension

- Your stomach knotting up

- Headache

- Joint pain

- An increase in heart rate and/or blood pressure

These physical symptoms may be caused and/or aggravated by your anger. Note how frequently the symptoms appear and, when they do appear, how intense—on a scale of one to ten with ten being practically unbearable—those symptoms are. It is your body. Learn to listen to it. Note: If any of these symptoms persist, consult your physician as they could be the result of other medical conditions.

TAPPING INTO THE POWER OF FORGIVENESS

How you see things makes all the difference in the world. Have you ever awakened from a bad dream and found yourself in a sweat with your heart beating rapidly? Perhaps a bear was chasing you. But, in reality, what had happened? Nothing. You were fast asleep, and no bear roamed your room.

That truth doesn't matter to your body, though, because your mind saw the bear as if it were actually there and signaled your body to react accordingly. Your heart rate shot up, and the fuel burning in your muscles produced heat, causing you to break out in a sweat.

To experience this mind/body interaction for yourself, squeeze your fist as hard as you can for five seconds. Ready? Ready? Begin squeezing—5 . . . 4 . . . 3 . . . 2 . . . 1 . . . stop.

What was happening in your body during those five seconds? You probably noticed that you clenched your jaw and tightened the muscles up your arm and even into your back. Did you notice that you held your breath? (You did! Who told you to do that?) You also slowed your digestion, released certain hormones into your bloodstream, increased your heart rate and blood pressure, altered your cholesterol levels, and even suppressed your immune system. You didn't know you did all these things, but that is precisely what your mind directed your body to do—all below your level of awareness.

People who are able and willing to forgive tend to be more satisfied with life.

— Gallup poll

Now repeat the experiment. Once again squeeze your fist as hard as you can, but now laugh at the same time. Ready? Begin squeezing and laughing—5 . . . 4 . . . 3 . . . 2 . . . 1 . . . stop.

Did you notice anything different? You didn't squeeze as hard, did you? And there was less tension in your body. You breathed, your body released different hormones, your heart rate and blood pressure did not increase as much, and your immune system may actually have benefited from the exercise. Even though you were using the same muscles in both experiments, you could not squeeze as hard while you were laughing. Even elite athletes, given squeeze meters that measure force in pounds per square inch, cannot squeeze as hard while they're laughing.

Forgiveness is a tool that, when used regularly, enables you to handle life rather than be overwhelmed by it.

Why is this so? Because the brain's message to the body is not clear. Your laughter confuses your mind, and it isn't sure whether to feel anger or happiness. So your mind can't send a clear message to your body. That's why, in the second experiment, your body reacted differently even though you consciously gave it the same message and used the same muscles.

OK, that's interesting, you might think, *but so what? Why is it important? And what connection to forgiveness does it have?*

The importance of this mind/body connection is suc-
cinctly expressed in the title of this chapter: "What You
Tell Yourself Can Kill You." If you don't get a handle on
your anger and instead continue to tell yourself sad stories about how someone has unfairly hurt you, your body
will pay the price—and that price can be very, very steep.

2. To determine whether you might have an anger
   problem, answer the following multiple-choice
   questions.

ANGER TEST

1. When you go through an express checkout lane in a
   grocery store, you:

   a. Count the number of items in the carts in front of
      you

   b. Think about what you will have for supper

2. When you're driving and someone pulls right in
   front of you, nearly forcing you off the road, you:

   a. Get on the horn and give that #*@%# driver a
      piece of your mind

   b. Are thankful that you gave yourself enough time
      so that you don't have to drive like that person

3. When you accidentally stub your big toe, you:

   a. Kick the object with your good foot

   b. Remind yourself to pay more attention to where you're walking

4. When you see people you don't like, you:

   a. Think of all the bad things each of them has done to you

   b. Remind yourself that they have their own struggles

5. You are more inclined to think about:

   a. People who have hurt you

   b. People who have helped you

6. When waiting for an elevator, you:

   a. Count how long it waits on each floor and wish people would hurry

   b. Talk to the person next to you until the elevator arrives

7. When you make a bad shot on the fairway, you:

   a. Throw your club down on the ground

   b. Analyze your swing to correct any errors

8. When someone doesn't arrive on time, you:

   a. Think of how inconsiderate that person was to keep you waiting

   b. Hope nothing bad happened to cause the delay

9. When somebody makes a joke at your expense, you:

   a. Fire back a put-down of your own

   b. Laugh at the humor

10. When you see a scratch on the side of your car, you:

    a. Scratch the car next to you

    b. Stop by a store to purchase touch-up paint

11. When you get angry, you:

    a. Throw things

    b. Talk about it

12. You most often see your parents as:

    a. Dysfunctional

    b. Human

Now count the number of *a*'s you marked. Here's what the results indicate:

- If you marked one to three *a*'s, you do well with your anger.

- If you marked no *a*'s, you may be in denial about your true feelings.

- If you marked between four and seven *a*'s, be aware that you will have difficulties with anger on occasion and pay careful attention to your moods.

- If you marked eight or more *a*'s, you have a problem with anger.

Anger kills. So, if you have an anger problem, you really do need to take care of it—and the sooner the better. And what better way to deal with it than to learn to practice forgiveness?

Revisiting Maria's Story

One weekend Todd and Maria attended a forgiveness seminar in their hometown. During one of the breaks, Maria approached the seminar leader and admitted her deep resentment and anger toward her husband. The leader encouraged her to seek professional help for her marriage as well as assistance in addressing the killer resentment that had built up in her over the years. Without such intervention, her physical and emotional deterioration would only continue.

Do unto others what you would have them do unto you.

— *The Golden Rule*

3. Do you think forgiveness would help release Maria from her stress and anger and even give her ulcers time to heal? Why or why not?

4. Todd never repented for his treatment of Maria, so should Maria forgive him? Why or why not?

5. What factors would you encourage Maria to look at as she considered whether to forgive Todd now or sometime in the future?

6. By the way, is *now* always the right time to forgive—or could there be legitimate reasons to wait until a future time? Explain your thoughts and give an example.

7. If Maria forgave Todd, does that mean she should continue to live with him under the same circumstances? Explain your answer.

8. What might forgiveness look like for Maria?

9. What advice would you give Maria to help her reframe her grievance story?

 10. Think of a person who has hurt you. What could—or will—you do to begin to change your perception of this snake in the grass?

*M*ary was very bright but socially awkward. She desperately wanted a lasting romantic relationship, but she had been unable to make it happen. Every time she met a man she liked, she slept with him during their first week of dating, and no relationship ever progressed beyond that point. When Mary pressed for something more in the relationship, the man quickly bolted.

Even after Mary identified this unhealthy pattern, she didn't know how to change her behavior. Ultimately she chalked up her problem to finding all the wrong men in all the wrong places.

After a year of therapy, Mary was referred to my forgiveness program, and there she got in touch with her deepest grievance story. It turned out that her father had molested her when she was a child. That explained why she had great trouble trusting men. At the same time that she didn't trust them, though, Mary so much wanted men to accept her that she traded first-date sex for their attention. That was the root of her cycle of quick sex, followed by a breakup, followed by a new sexual partner.

In order to let go of her past and move on with her future—and away from this relational pattern that had developed—Mary needed to forgive her father. But this would not be an easy journey, for what he did to her could not be excused. She could not significantly reframe her father's behavior—he did what he did. Nevertheless Mary did begin to see many things in a very different light. For instance, she no longer *saw her father as the authority figure, but as a weak man powerless to control his dark impulses. She also saw how her childhood experience caused her to seek attention in unhealthy ways. And she realized that she could learn to enjoy conversation without having to hook someone into a relationship too soon. She learned to become more patient with friendship and worked on being less needy and intense.*

What You Need to Know

Forgiveness releases you from the hurts of your past so that you can energetically pursue the future you desire for yourself. Forgiveness enables you to leave behind "if only . . ." thinking ("If only I had studied more while I was in school . . .") for hope-filled "what if . . . ?" thoughts ("What if I take a night class this semester?").

And since you become what you spend the majority of your time thinking about, wouldn't you rather concentrate on positive, future-oriented thoughts instead of negative, backward-looking ones? In order to do that, however, you need to know where you want to go.

So how does forgiveness not only free you from a dark and unproductive past, but also encourage you to reach for a bright, fulfilling future? It does so partly by encouraging you to set goals for yourself. You probably know the old saying: "What you can conceive, you can achieve." Goals enable you to conceive of the particular steps it will take in order for you to reach your desired destination. Attainable, realistic goals have five characteristics:

There can be no future without forgiveness.

— Desmond Tutu

- *Written.* Goals become real only when you write them down. If you don't put your goals in writing, they will remain vague wishes of what might be.

- *Specific*. The clearer the goal, the easier it is to determine exactly what you need to do to get there.

- *Sequenced*. The more specifically you define each step you need to take to achieve your goals, the easier it will be for you to do so.

- *Measurable*. Make sure that progress toward your goals can be measured and then find a practical way to track that progress.

- *Scheduled*. Helpful goals specify some kind of completion date. They do not hang out there somewhere to be completed "someday."

Forgiveness is what allows wounded people to let go of yesterday and build tomorrow.

Your ability to achieve your goals is all but guaranteed if you take small steps toward those goals each and every day. You achieve success one step at a time. That's why I strongly encourage you to categorize your goals as short-term goals (these can be completed in a day, a week, or a month), intermediate goals (these may take one to three years to complete), and long-term goals (you'll work toward these for more than three years). Every day you should be taking small steps to achieve your goals. (For further assistance in setting helpful goals, see chapter 10 in the book *Forgive to Live*).

Reaching your goals is all about living life according to your priorities; it's about not letting urgent matters crowd out the important ones. Life is often a juggling act, and everyone lets a few balls drop to the ground at some point. Just make sure the balls you drop are never the most important ones; the others will eventually come bouncing back.

Finally, to have the most satisfying life possible, let one of your most important goals be to make forgiveness a habitual part of your life. Martin Luther King Jr. once said, "Forgiveness is not an occasional act; it is a permanent attitude." The ultimate goal, then, is to move from forgiveness as a tactic for coping with a specific conflict to forgiveness as a strategy for living.

Where there is hatred, let me sow love; where there is injury, pardon . . . For it is in giving that we receive; it is in pardoning that we are pardoned.

— St. Francis of Assisi

Forgiveness can be seen as either a *state* or a *trait*. The latter tends to grow out of the former. *State* forgiveness is something you do in response to an unwanted situation. *Trait* forgiveness is a part of who you are; it's a characteristic, an integral component of who you are. The final phase of forgiveness involves moving from state forgiveness to trait forgiveness. The transition happens once you stop seeing forgiveness as a tool for coping with a particular conflict or crisis and instead make it the way you live life every day.

And why is a lifestyle of forgiveness important? A recent Gallup poll reports that people who are able and willing to forgive tend to be more satisfied with life. Do you want more satisfaction in life? Then work on making forgiveness a permanent part of your life (for assistance in how to do this, see chapter 12 of the book *Forgive to Live*).

The fact is, the more important forgiveness is to you, the more likely you are to forgive. And the more often you practice forgiveness, the more forgiving you will become. Best of all, perhaps, a forgiving orientation reduces the number of times you'll have to forgive in the first place. When you fully realize that you always have the option to forgive, you also realize that you have the choice *not* to take offense in the first place. Also, since you know life *isn't* fair, you won't expect it to be—and that means you'll get hurt less often.

Forgiveness has the power to turn pessimists into optimists. It helps the forgiver to see the world differently, to gain a new perspective on life. Circumstances, relationships, jobs—any and every aspect of life really can get better.

Now consider this important point: forgiveness is ultimately a spiritual journey. Let me explain by first saying that your character—who you are at the deepest level—is shaped by your values and purpose in life. The choices you make and the actions that follow speak volumes about who you really are. Character is far more important than who you know or what you do—and forgiveness is a clear and visible way of demonstrating the strength of your character. Your ability to forgive in different situations reveals your spiritual nature. Your willingness to forgive makes this a better world, not only for you, but for all those around you.

Spiritual individuals recognize that nothing needs to chain them to the past and that they have the opportunity and ability to live for tomorrow. They see eternal significance in the temporal and thus have the broadest frame of reference in which to place their life. Spiritual individuals live each day in the context of a greater purpose in life.

Spiritual individuals also understand that living with an eye toward possibilities is much more rewarding than living preoccupied with one's problems. They can't understand why anyone would choose to remain trapped in the troubles of their yesterdays when a whole lifetime of dazzling tomorrows beckons. So, through forgiveness, spiritual individuals let go and move on.

During interviews at the end of my forgiveness training classes, I invite participants to describe what they found most helpful in their sessions. Each time I expect them to say something like "I feel good about being able to reduce my anger" or "I was delighted to lower my blood pressure." Instead, they most often say something like "I now have a spiritual awakening in my life. For the first time ever, I feel that my life has direction and purpose. I feel like I'm getting back on track to where my life should have always been." Even though people who practice forgiveness experience significant mental and physical benefits, the majority of study participants said they felt most thankful for the *spiritual* benefits of forgiveness.

Eighteenth-century Dutch physician Paul Boese beautifully summed up the amazing power of forgiveness:

If you first get the big things, the truly important things, in place in your life, there will always be room for the other things. But if you first try to get all the little things done, there will never be room for the larger, more important things.

"Forgiveness does not change the past," he said, "but it does enlarge the future."

And it will enlarge your future too.

Tapping Into the Power of Forgiveness

In the game of life, nobody bats a thousand. We all make mistakes. How you handle those mistakes and how you forgive those who hurt you makes all the difference in the world.

Mahatma Gandhi once said, "The weak can never forgive. Forgiveness is the attribute of the strong." Later he went on to say, "If we practice an eye for an eye and a tooth for a tooth, soon the whole world will be blind and toothless."

We must develop and maintain the capacity to forgive. He who is devoid of the power to forgive is devoid of the power to love.

— Dr. Martin Luther King Jr.

If you don't forgive, you may come to hate everyone who has hurt you. Or you may withdraw from life because you see the world as a very pain-filled place to live. The healthier alternative is to forgive—and the choice is completely yours.

1. Now, to determine where you are on your forgiveness journey, answer the following ten questions as honestly as you can.

THE FORGIVENESS JOURNEY

	YES	NO
1. Do you have a story about someone who has wronged you, someone whom you have yet to forgive?	___	___
2. Are you aware of the price you are paying by not forgiving?	___	___
3. Have you made the choice to forgive?	___	___
4. Are you able to sufficiently change your story of hurt and suffering so it is less painful?	___	___
5. Has your new story of the old event given you a better perspective on life?	___	___
6. When a situation brings you back to feeling helpless, are you able to change that feeling?	___	___
7. Are you making progress toward achieving the goals you have set for yourself?	___	___

8. Are you more understanding of the other
    person's circumstances even though you
    disagree with what he or she did?   ___ ___

9. Have you reconciled with the person
    involved?   ___ ___

10. Has forgiveness brought you peace with
    God or greater clarity about your higher
    purpose in life?   ___ ___

Spiritual individuals live each day in the context of a greater purpose in life.

Don't be concerned if you were unable to answer yes to all ten questions. The journey to making forgiveness a habit for life happens one step at a time, and you're on your way.

REVISITING MARY'S STORY

Forgiveness helped Mary break free from her past and set a different course for her future. Rather than making her father the main character in her story, she took control of her life. In time Mary began to see a brighter future for herself, one where she really could develop a successful romantic relationship. Every day she practiced letting go of her past and taking steps toward the future she desired, and soon that healthy mind-set became a habit for her.

By uncovering her grievance story, framing it differently, and using new insights to adjust her expectations of herself and others, Mary finally broke free from unhealthy ways of relating to men. She established certain standards for building solid relationships. For example, she made a commitment not to seek anything more than friendship during the first three months of dating someone. After that period, if anything more serious seemed possible, the couple would sit down to discuss their future together and to identify the goals and values they shared. Eventually Mary found a wonderful man—and after dating for two years, the couple got married.

The only effective response to the past is forgiveness, the only effective response to the present is love, and the only effective response to the future is hope.

2. Is your life today free from the entrapment of the past, or are you still living in your painful yesterday? Explain.

3. What goals have you set for yourself that will guide your choices and actions over the next week, months, and years? List your short-term, intermediate, and long-term goals. If you haven't set goals for yourself, why haven't you?

4. Short-term and intermediate goals should move us toward achieving our long-term goals. What are you doing *today* to move one step closer to fulfilling your goals? Be specific.

5. What tends to keep you from achieving goals that you set for yourself? What might forgiveness do to reduce those barriers?

6. What can you do to keep the urgent from crowding out the important in your life?

7. What practical steps can you take to keep a fear of failure from allowing you to move ahead toward your desired future? Be specific.

8. What is the difference between forgiveness as a *tactic* for dealing with a specific problem and forgiveness as a *strategy* for dealing with life in general?

9. What can you do to make forgiveness a permanent attitude, a foundational principle of your life, a trait of your character? Be specific.

10. Explain why practicing forgiveness reduces the frequency you'll have to forgive in the first place.

11. Why does forgiving become easier with practice?

12. Explain why forgiveness is ultimately a spiritual journey.

13. Why does forgiveness give you the ability to live for tomorrow?

APPENDIX: TIPS FOR LEADING A DISCUSSION

Your role in *Forgive to Live* is key! After all, your job as a discussion leader is to encourage members of your group to think about what they are studying, talk about what they're learning, and discover ways to apply those lessons to their life. That is what the questions in the workbook—those flagged throughout with —are designed to do.

As members in your group grapple with both the meaning and application of the material, it is important that they feel comfortable expressing their opinions and ideas. One way to set that tone is to make clear that there is no single correct response to each question. (Besides, discussions will be richer when many different views are shared.) So be careful not to judge someone's response as either right or wrong. Instead, accept the different points of view. If you are uncomfortable with a particular response, ask further questions in order to determine what the person really means.

Also remember that your role as leader is one of coach and facilitator. It is better for people to discover answers on their own rather than to merely buy into your answer. You are not to have all the answers, or people will look to you to answer the questions rather than wrestle with the issues themselves. You should take comfort in the fact that you are not expected to have all the answers

Be enthusiastic about people's responses and participation. We all are more engaged in a conversation when we believe that what we have to

offer is valued and contributes to the thinking of everyone else in the group.

In order to maximize the effectiveness of discussion
time, consider these tips:

- Insist that everything that is shared be kept strictly
  confidential. This guarantee is essential to making
  the group safe.

- Remind group members that time is limited so, when
  they're talking, to be careful not to monopolize the
  minutes. Everyone needs to share! Also be aware of
  people's hidden agendas. They can use any topic to
  talk about what they want to discuss. If this occurs,
  you may want to say something like: "Let's hold that
  thought for a while and stay with this topic."

- Sit right next to the talkative people so that they
  have a harder time making eye contact with you
  and therefore may not speak as much. Sit across
  from people who need to be encouraged to share.
  Your eye contact may help draw them out. (Yes, you
  are helping your group members share the time!)

- Get to know your group and choose ahead of time
  those questions that you feel will be most helpful
  and productive.

- Affirm people as they share answers. Validate members who take the risk of being honest and vulnerable.

- Ask for clarification when appropriate. Repeat the person's answer in your own words to show that you were listening and truly want to understand.

- Keep the conversation moving, but don't be afraid of silence between your reading of the question and the first response. Those few quiet seconds will seem longer to you than to anyone else. If those few seconds become several seconds, rephrase the question or perhaps even move on.

- There may be a few silent members in your group. Don't single them out and comment that they have not said anything. Instead, watch for their facial or body gestures and then say something like: "You look like you agree with that. Do you?" Then thank them for their response. Positive reinforcement goes a long way.

Also, here are some helpful statements to have in your back pocket.

- "Tanya, you've contributed some great thoughts tonight, but there may be others who have something to say. Let's give them a chance to speak, and then I'll come back to you, OK?" (And be sure to get back to Tanya!)

- "Great insight, Ron! Thanks for sharing!"

- "Do I have your meaning right? Correct me if I don't."

- "Could we return to the point that was made earlier?"

- "Let's pursue that topic a little more."

Finally, keep in mind that the leader often learns more than the participants. So relax and enjoy learning from them. They don't expect you to have all the answers, so don't put that pressure on yourself. Instead, sit back and be amazed at how many good ideas emerge from members of your group.

Thanks for your willingness to lead a group discussion. I trust your experience will be personally rewarding as you see group members help one another find the freedom and life that come with forgiving.

Dick Tibbits

ABOUT THE AUTHOR

Dr. Dick Tibbits has worked in the field of pastoral care and behavioral health for more than thirty years. He has used his training and experience in counseling to help tens of thousands of people achieve a better life. Dr. Tibbits has dedicated his life to whole-person health and designing life strategies that work in both the corporate world and private life.

Dr. Tibbits has a doctoral degree in psychology and is a licensed professional counselor. He is also an ordained minister with a master's degree in theology. He has served as an adjunct professor for doctoral students at both Fuller Theological Seminary and Andrews University Theological Seminary. Dr. Tibbits is a certified supervisor with the Association for Clinical Pastoral Education. In addition, Dr. Tibbits trained at the Harvard University Mind-Body-Spirit Institute and worked collaboratively with professors from Stanford University on his pioneering clinical research.

Dr. Tibbits has spoken on the healing power of forgiveness to professional and private audiences around the world, including Australia, New Zealand, Hong Kong, the Philippines, India, and Switzerland. He has presented his research at Harvard, Mayo, Stanford, and Loma Linda as well as to conferences as diverse as The International Conference on Stress and The National Woman's Health Conference. He has appeared on a number of radio and TV talk shows.

Dr. Tibbits currently serves as the Chief People Officer at Florida Hospital, the largest hospital in America.

To find out more about Dr. Tibbits's work, please visit him online at:

www.DickTibbits.com

FLORIDA HOSPITAL

For nearly one hundred years, the mission of Florida Hospital has been to help patients, guests, and friends achieve whole-person health and healing. With seven hospital campuses and sixteen walk-in medical centers, Florida Hospital cares for nearly one million patients every year.

Over a decade ago Florida Hospital began working with the Disney Corporation to create a groundbreaking facility that would showcase the model of health care for the twenty-first century and stay on the cutting edge of medical technology as it develops. A team of medical experts, industry leaders, and health-care futurists designed and built a whole-person health hospital named Celebration Health located in Disney's town of Celebration, Florida. Since opening its doors in 1997, Celebration Health has been awarded the Premier Patient Services Innovator Award as "The Model for Health-Care Delivery in the 21st Century."

When Dr. Lydia Parmele, the first female physician in the state of Florida, and her medical team opened Florida Hospital in 1908, their goal was to create a healing environment where they not only treated illness but also provided the support and education necessary to help patients achieve mental, physical, spiritual, and social health—or, simply put, whole-person health.

The lifestyle advocated by Florida Hospital founders remains central to carrying out that mission today. Patients learn how to reduce the risk of disease through healthy lifestyle choices, and they are encouraged to use natural remedies such as fresh air, sunshine, water, rest, nutrition, exercise, outlook, faith, and interpersonal relationships.

Today, Florida Hospital:

- Is ranked by the American Hospital Association as number one in the nation for inpatient admissions

- Is the largest provider of Medicare services in the country

- Performs the most heart procedures each year, making the number one hospital the leader in fighting America's number one killer—heart disease

- Operates many nationally recognized centers of excellence including Cardiology, Cancer, Orthopedics, Neurology & Neurosurgery, Digestive Disorders, and Minimally Invasive Surgery

- Is, according to *Fit Pregnancy* magazine, one of the "Top 10 Best Places in the Country to Have a Baby"

For more information about Florida Hospital and whole-person health products including books, music, videos, conferences, seminars, and other resources, please contact:

Florida Hospital Publishing
683 Winyah Drive, Orlando, FL 32803
Phone: 407-303-7711 • Fax: 407-303-1818
Email: healthproducts@flhosp.org
www.FloridaHospital.com • www.CreationHealth.com

Forgive to Live

HOW FORGIVENESS CAN SAVE YOUR LIFE.

We either become overwhelmed by life's difficulties or we become strengthened by life's hardest lessons. The difference is found in one's ability to forgive. Dr. Dick Tibbits shows you how forgiveness can effectively reduce your anger, drastically improve your health and put you in charge of your life again, no matter how deep your hurt.

AS YOU:

- come to a new understanding of what has happened to you.
  - discover what forgiveness does and doesn't mean.
  - take steps to reframe your grievance story.
  - stop giving control to the people and pains of the past.
  - get your life — and maybe even your health — back.
- find a freedom, peace…and strength you've never had.

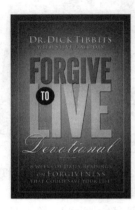